W9-CXT-236

North America

by Katie Bagley

Consultant:
Catherine H. Helgeland
Professor of Geography
University of Wisconsin–Manitowoc
Manitowoc, Wisconsin

Bridgestone Books
an imprint of Capstone Press
Mankato, Minnesota

Bridgestone Books are published by Capstone Press
151 Good Counsel Drive, P.O. Box 669, Mankato, Minnesota 56002
http://www.capstone-press.com

Printed in the United States of America.

Library of Congress Cataloging-in-Publication Data
Bagley, Katie.
North America/by Katie Bagley.
p. cm.—(Continents)
Summary: Describes the regions, landforms, people, and interesting places of the North American continent.
Includes bibliographical references and index.
ISBN 0-7368-1419-1 (hardcover)
1. North America—Juvenile literature. [1. North America.] I. Title. II. Continents (Mankato, Minn.)
E38.5 .B34 2003
917—dc21 2001008089

Editorial Credits
Erika Mikkelson, editor; Karen Risch, product planning editor; Linda Clavel, designer and illustrator; Image Select International, photo researchers

Photo Credits
Art Directors and TRIP/N. Wiseman, 22 (Grand Canyon); M. Cerny, 22 (volcano)
CORBIS/Paul A. Sonders, 13; Earl and Nazima Kowall, 18; Charles Mauzy, 20; John Conrad, 21
Digital Stock, 15
Digital Vision, 17
Digital Wisdom/Mountain High, cover
Don Stevenson/Indexstock Imagery/PictureQuest, 19
Eyewire, 11
Masterfile, 22 (Lake Superior)

1 2 3 4 5 6 07 06 05 04 03 02

Table of Contents

Fast Facts about North America

Size: 9,361,791 square miles (24,247,039 square kilometers)

Number of countries: 24

Population: 481 million (early 2000s estimate)

Highest point: Mount McKinley, Alaska, 20,320 feet (6,194 meters) above sea level

Lowest point: Death Valley, California, 282 feet (86 meters) below sea level

Largest cities: Mexico City, Mexico; New York City, United States; Toronto, Canada

Longest river: Mississippi River, 2,357 miles (3,793 kilometers) long

Countries in North America

1. Canada
2. United States
3. Greenland (belongs to Denmark)
4. Mexico
5. Bahamas
6. Cuba
7. Jamaica
8. Haiti
9. Dominican Republic
10. Panama
11. Costa Rica
12. Nicaragua
13. Honduras
14. El Salvador
15. Guatemala
16. Belize
17. St. Kitts-Nevis
18. Antigua and Barbuda
19. Dominica
20. Barbados
21. St. Lucia
22. St. Vincent and the Grenadines
23. Grenada
24. Trinidad and Tobago

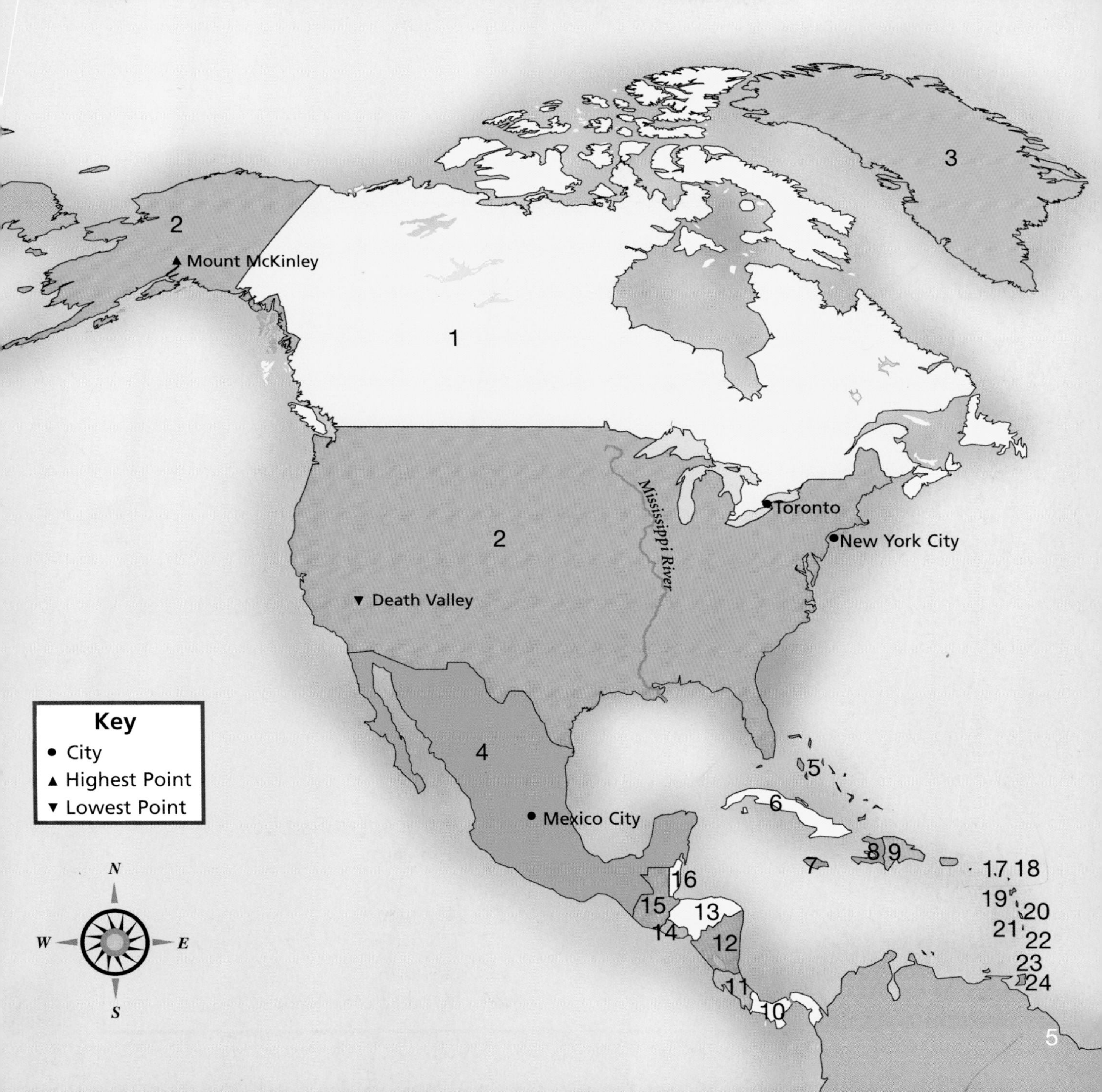
3
2
Mount McKinley
1
Mississippi River
Toronto
2
New York City
Death Valley
Key
City
Highest Point
Lowest Point
4
Mexico City
5
6
7
8
9
17
18
16
19
15
13
20
14
21
12
22
23
11
24
10
N
W
E
S

North America

North America is the third largest continent. The Arctic Ocean lies to its north. The Atlantic Ocean is to the east. The Pacific Ocean is to the west. The Gulf of Mexico and the Caribbean Sea lie to the south. An isthmus connects North America to South America.

isthmus

a narrow strip of land that lies between two bodies of water and connects two larger landmasses

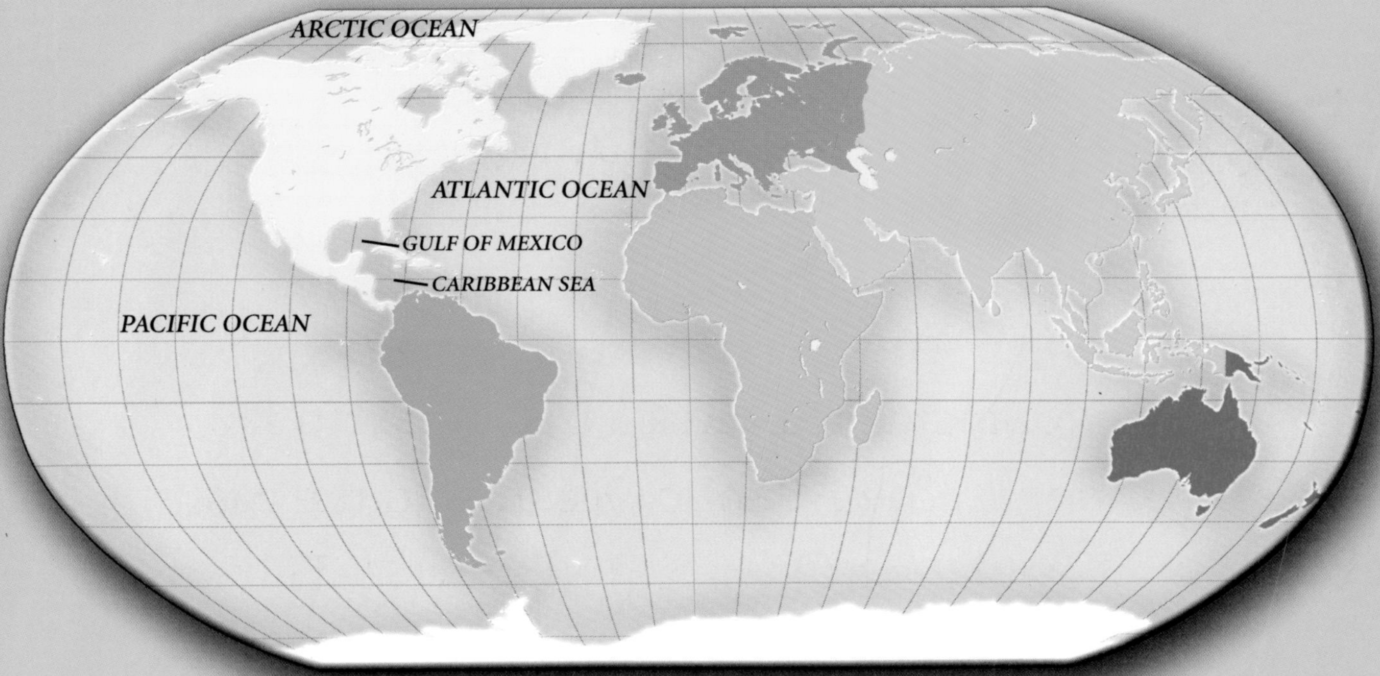

ARCTIC OCEAN
ATLANTIC OCEAN
GULF OF MEXICO
CARIBBEAN SEA
PACIFIC OCEAN

Key
Africa
Antarctica
Asia
Australia
Europe
North America
South America
N
W
E
S

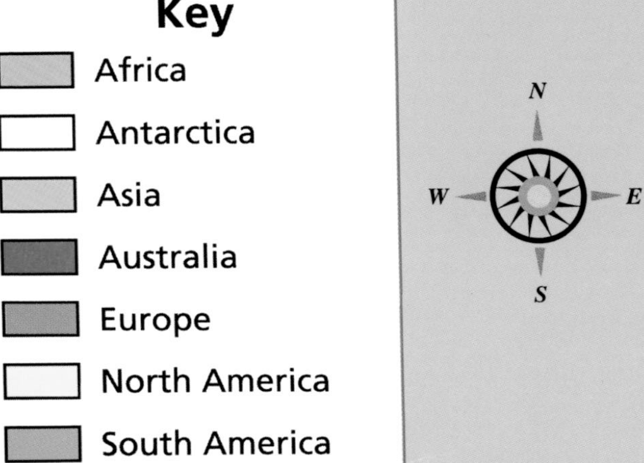

North America's Land

North America has mountains along its eastern and western sides. Some of the western mountains are volcanoes. Low hills and plateaus lie in central North America. This area contains the world's oldest rocks. Geologists have found rocks in northern Canada that are about 4 billion years old.

geologist
a scientist who studies the history of the earth through rocks

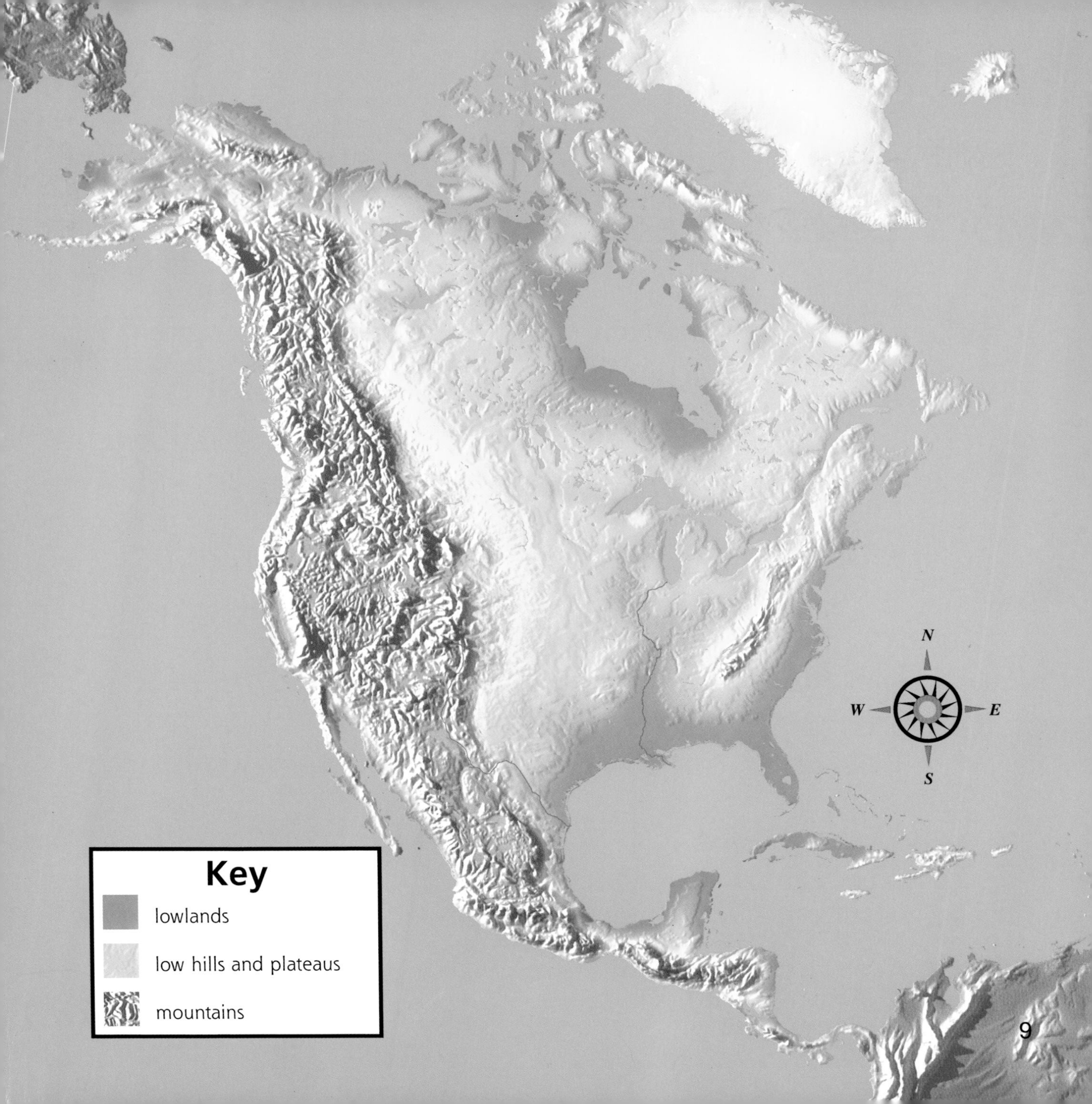
Key
lowlands
low hills and plateaus
mountains
N
W
E
S

Western North America

Several mountain ranges are in western North America. The Cascade Mountains and the Sierra Nevadas are near the west coast.

Rocky Mountains

The Rocky Mountains lie farther to the east. Plateaus and basins lie between the mountains on the west coast and the Rocky Mountains.

basin
a low, bowl-shaped area in the surface of the Earth

Central North America

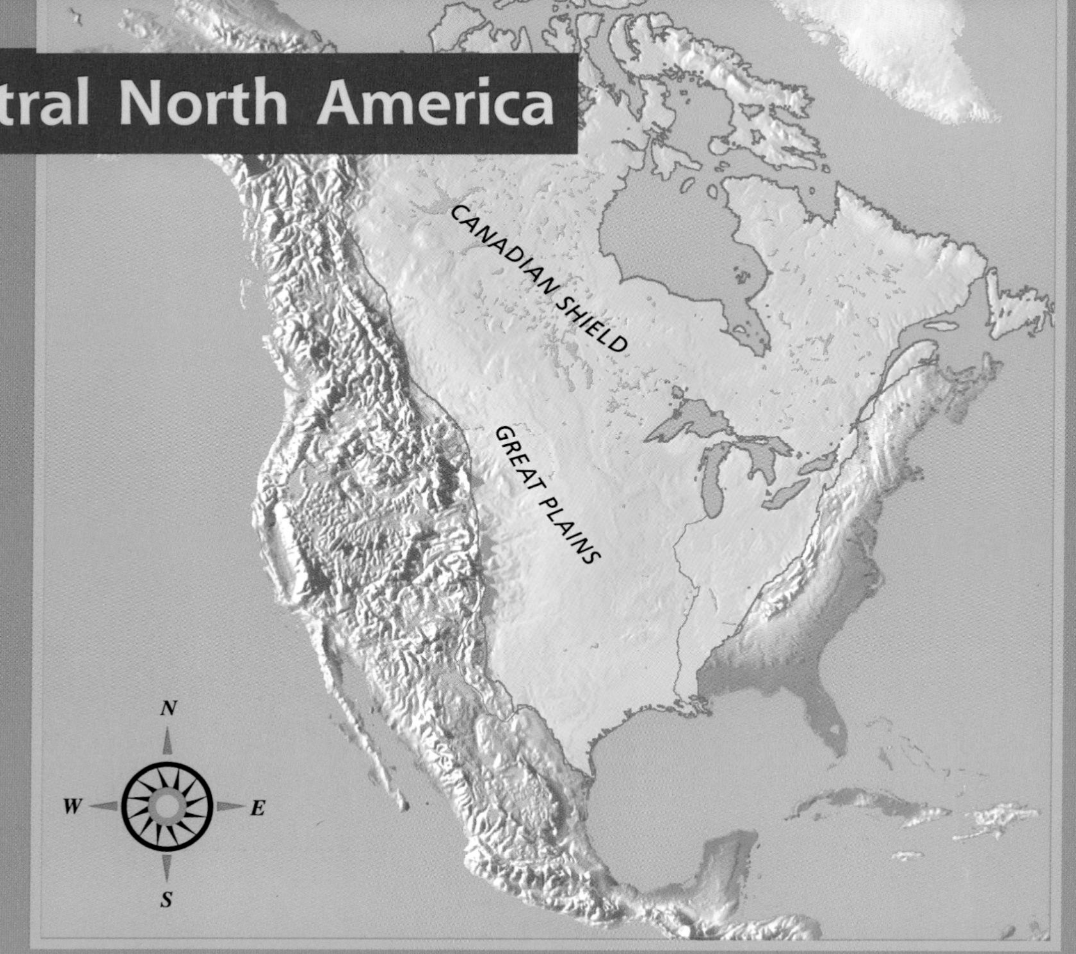

Central North America is mostly flat. The Canadian Shield covers most of northern Canada. Ancient rock makes up this huge, flat area.

ancient
from a long time ago

wheat field

The Great Plains lie south of the Canadian Shield. The soil in the Great Plains is good for growing crops.

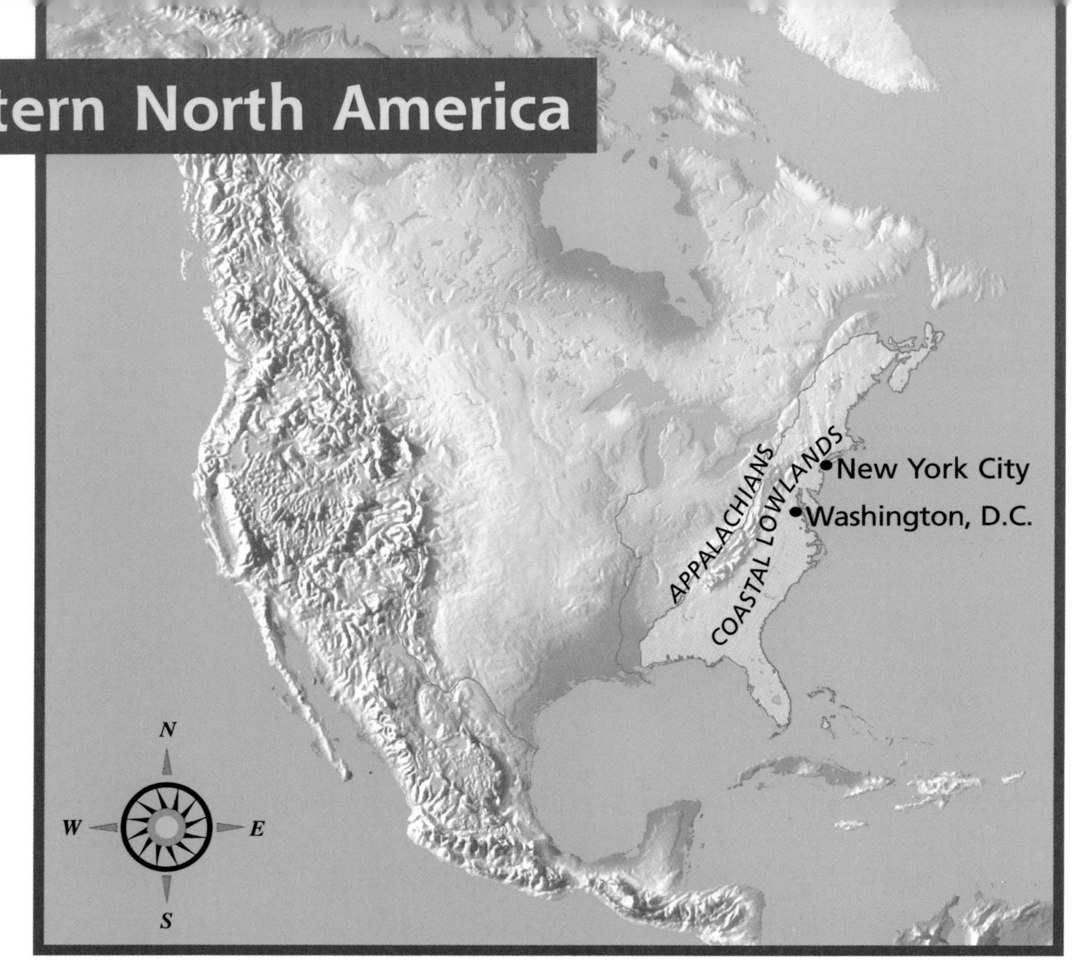

The Appalachian Mountains divide the eastern region from the central region. These low, rounded mountains are covered with trees.

Washington, D.C.

East of the Appalachians are the coastal lowlands. New York City and Washington, D.C., are found on the coastal lowlands.

coastal lowland
a flat area of land near an ocean

Central America

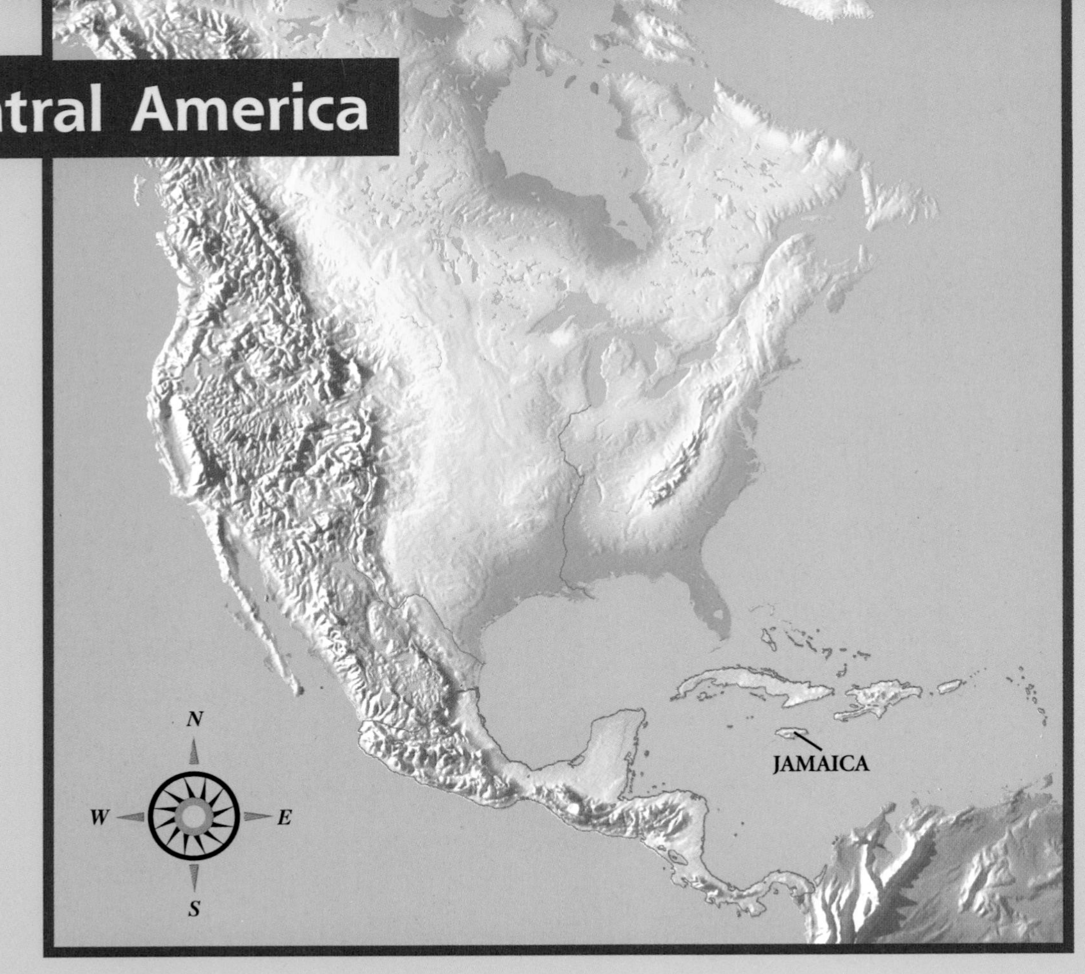

Central America is an isthmus that connects Mexico and South America. A chain of volcanoes runs through Central America.

Jamaica

Volcanoes form most of the islands in the Caribbean Sea. Islands in the Caribbean Sea are popular places for tourists to visit.

North America's People

Scientists think people first came to North America from Asia. They arrived between 15,000 and 35,000 years ago.

Many Europeans came to North America in the 1800s. People from Africa, Asia, and South America also live in North America.

North America's Animals

caribou

Many kinds of animals live in North America. Caribou live in the northern areas of the continent.

caribou
a large deer; people also call caribou reindeer.

cougar

Bears are found throughout North America. Cougars live in the mountains. Many types of fish swim in North America's waters.

Reading Maps: North America's Sights to See

1. The Grand Canyon is more than 1 mile (1,609 meters) deep. Look at the map on page 5. In what country is the Grand Canyon found? If you were traveling from Mexico, which direction would you go to find the Grand Canyon?

2. Lake Superior is the largest freshwater lake in the world. It is one of the five Great Lakes in North America. Look at the map on page 7. In which direction would you travel to get to the Atlantic Ocean?

3. Popocatépetl (POH-poh-kah-te-pet-ul) is one of the most active volcanoes in Mexico. Popocatépetl last erupted in September 2000. Look at the map on page 7. Which direction would you travel to get from Popocatépetl to the Caribbean Sea?

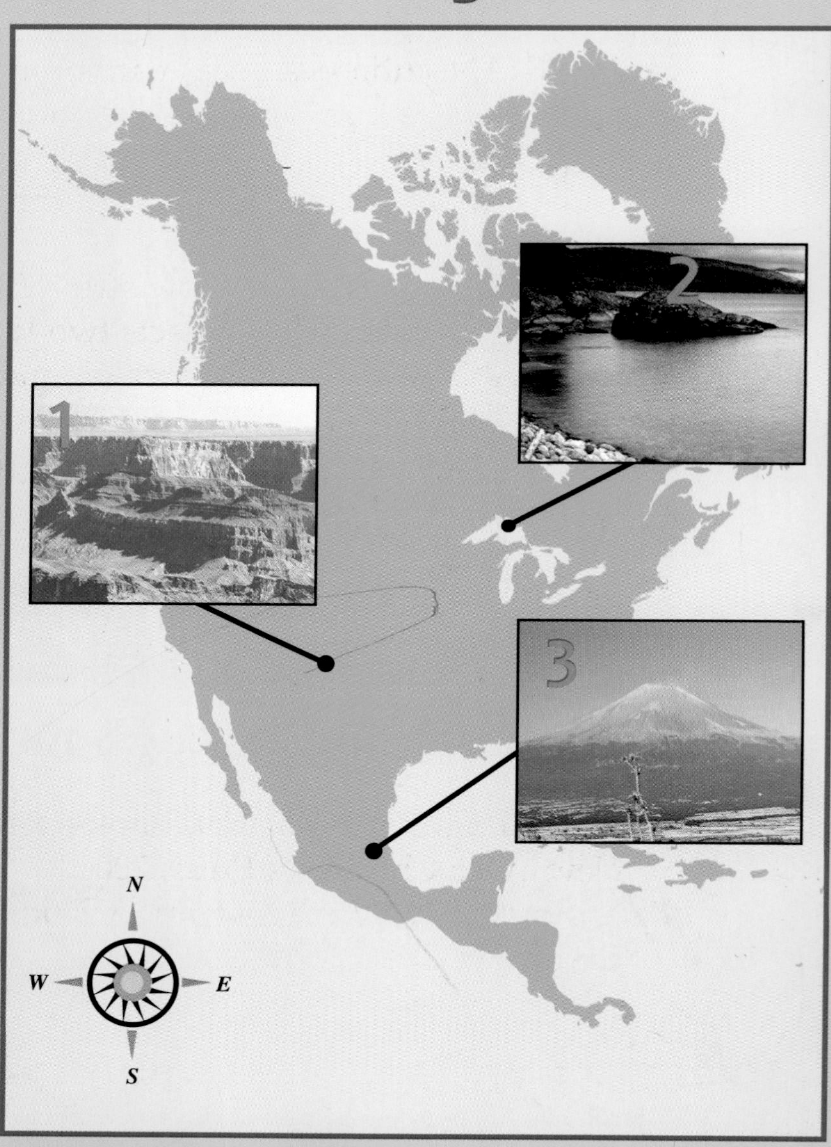

Words to Know

canyon (KAN-yuhn)—a deep, narrow area with steep sides; a canyon often has a stream or a river running through it.

connect (kuh-NEKT)—to join together two or more places

continent (KON-tuh-nuhnt)—one of the seven main landmasses of Earth

isthmus (ISS-muhss)—a narrow strip of land that lies between two bodies of water and connects two larger landmasses

plain (PLANE)—a large, flat area of land

plateau (plah-TOH)—a raised area of flat land

range (RAYNJ)—a chain or large group of mountains

volcano (vol-KAY-noh)—a mountain with vents; a vent is a passage that goes deep into Earth; melted rock, ash, and gases erupt through the vents.

Read More

Fowler, Allan. *North America.* Rookie Read-About Geography. New York: Children's Press, 2001.

Petersen, David. *North America.* A True Book. New York: Children's Press, 1998.

Internet Sites

NationalGeographic.com—Map Machine
http://plasma.nationalgeographic.com/mapmachine/facts_fs.html
WorldAtlas.com—North America
http://www.graphicmaps.com/webimage/countrys/na.htm

Index